LCKDOWN

LIFE

By
Daniella Blechner

Humour

Lockdown Life

Copyright © 2020 Daniella Blechner

First printed in United Kingdom, 2020.

Published by Conscious Dreams Publishing.
www.consciousdreamspublishing.com

Edited by Rhoda Molife and Lee Dickinson.

Typeset by Oksana Kosovan

Illustrations by imaginabox studio and Rahmon

Cover Art by Jae Thompson

Book Cover by Alaka Oladimeji Basit

ISBN: 978-1-913674-16-8

Dedicated

to Humanity, with Love and Humour

Acknowledgements

In and amongst the confusion and uncertainty, a great deal of us have lost loved ones, worried about loved ones and been in permanent carer mode for so many. My heart and love go out to you.

My heart, love and respect goes out to NHS workers – doctors and nurses, admin, cleaners – those on the front line and those behind the scenes who get up every day to serve.

My love goes out to the key workers: carers who look after the elderly and vulnerable and teachers who keep the children of key workers and vulnerable children safe and well at school whilst engaging them in activities they enjoy, grow and learn from.

My love goes out all those who gave up their time to serve the community during this time. Shout out to Lawrence Coke who was a pillar in the community delivering food and essentials like a superhero to those that needed it. Shout out to Mackaylah Forde assisting people at food banks. Shout out to Tania Pinnock who cooked and provided tasty Caribbean delights across London. Shout out to Donna Murray-Turner, Founder of ANOS, an organisation dedicated to serving the community. Shout out to Emma, Steve and Keira who coordinated the Covid 19 Mutal Aid volunteer team in Gipsy Hill. And a huge shout out to Natasha Benjamin, Founder of Free Your Mind CIC, who provided invaluable support to children affected by Domestic Violence during this time.

My heart goes out to anyone stuck in toxic and abusive relationships. I want you to know you are loved, and you are stronger than you will ever know. I pray that one day you will see the treatment you receive is not a reflection of who you are or what you deserve, but of their inadequacy. Leaving takes courage and it will be the most loving thing you can ever do for yourself.

My heart goes out to the lonely and vulnerable, those self-isolating alone and battling things we may never hear about, to those who are anxious, depressed or living in fear and to our elderly neighbours whose only interaction comes through speaking to strangers and community support. When this is over, I will make an effort to love you just that little bit more.

I see and acknowledge you all.

A percentage of the proceeds of this book will go towards supporting Free Your Mind CIC supporting children affected by Domestic Violence.

Introduction

The world is on lockdown. It's as though we've all been sent to our rooms without really understanding what we've done. Some have panicked, bought enough toilet paper to build an empire – cleaning out the supermarket shelves like they were on an episode of *Supermarket Sweep*, whilst others have opened their hearts to the community, understanding that we co-exist as a collective.

Some of us have experienced more emotions than rainy days in the UK, in the space of a single day, causing family members and friends to wonder if they could include a split personality test in their next online shop! Amidst the chaos, a good number of us have tried to find some peace. Some of us have prayed fervently to our God, others have drunk cacao on a full moon, creating quiet ceremonies alone in their homes, hoping to receive downloads and insights about the next step for humanity, whilst others have had to buy human wedges to force themselves out of their sofas, having rinsed out their Netflix accounts.

Entrepreneurs and self-employed people were forced to navigate their way around the government funding and guidelines as if trying to get out of the Escape Room on *The Crystal Maze*! Some have pushed hard to make their businesses work, telling everyone to 'revolutionise their business', and life coaches sang that we must 'pursue new hobbies' (albeit some of them with their dressing gowns on behind a laptop in bed). Others could barely drag themselves out of bed or tell you what day of the week it was. A lot of us will come out of this bi- or tri-lingual and some will quit their corporate jobs to lead meditation retreats or sell paintings for £10k instead!

2020 will be known as the year when words such as 'social distancing' 'self-isolation' and 'quarantine' became the norm, but I wanted to add a few more of my own. In this book, you'll discover the complete guide to essential 'lockdown language' that'll allow you to have those much-needed conversations (through Zoom or Houseparty) with friends and loved ones who truly understand the life. It's a comprehensive 'how-to' on handling the pushy entrepreneur on social, the young couple who cross the road when they see you and avoid eye contact and the 'roadman' who's been waiting outside Costcutter for pretty women to pop out and get some toilet roll.

This book is written with love and humour. Duality has existed since the beginning of time. We cannot have chaos without order or tragedy without laughter. Laughter is medicine. It's the river that runs through all things. We can find beauty in the struggle and light and laughter in the darkness. I hope that in these times, this book brings you a little relief from whatever you're going through and spreads a little joy and humour into your life.

Contents

Lockdown Life

Lockdown Life refers to the time in our lives when we were given specific instruction to stay at home to in order to save lives. Now this was met with an array of emotions. Whilst many introverts danced with glee in the comfort of their homes, extroverts felt as if the rug had been pulled out from under their feet as they struggled to see how they could survive without a full diary of social gatherings. Some of us, myself included, lost one or two jobs in one day and were overwhelmed with thoughts of how to stay financially solvent and stable in a hostile climate. Many of us wondered how we'd support our families as the life we'd known crumbled beneath our feet.

Before lockdown was announced, some of us felt it coming, made provisions and stocked up, and some even went as far as driving back home to their families in the countryside hoping the endless green fields would protect them from threat.

When the lockdown was announced, it was almost as though God had put a pause button on our decisions. Whoever we were with or whatever we were doing at that very moment was a clear reflection of our life choices and we'd been given an opportunity to face those choices. Newly formed romances and couples made rushed commitments to move in together, situationships faded away (or not), couples on the verge of break-up were given an opportunity to have free couples' therapy, which meant facing issues they'd ignored without having anywhere to run to except to the local shop and back, or to the spare room if leaving the house wasn't an option. Sadly, some were trapped indoors with their perpetrators, making escaping abuse a near impossibility. My heart goes out to the many women, children and men who've been affected by domestic violence.

A proportion of the proceeds from this book will go towards Free Your Mind CIC whose mission is to support individuals that have experienced domestic violence and mental illness as a result. *www.freeyourmindcic.com*

LOCKDOWN

PERSONALITIES

Lockdown Extros

The Lockdown Extros are those that shine in public. Their life is lived through social events and gatherings and they're often the life and soul of the party. Lockdown Extros rarely spend time at home; in fact, they couldn't tell you the last time they spent more than 24 hours inside it. They can often be found by their windows trying

to catch a glimpse of freedom, whilst others are constantly on their mobiles chatting to everybody and anybody at any time. Extros dominate Houseparty, inviting and connecting strange mixes of new colleagues and old-skool friends and family members whether they like it or not, creating awkward social mixing experiments.

How to Spot an Extro

Key phrases: 'When I used to have a life …'; 'I feel like I'm a prisoner in my own home'; 'Let's organise a group call, babe'.

Demeanour: A permanent look of panic and a faraway gaze to the days BL (Before Lockdown) when the diary was full.

Lockdown Intros

Lockdown Intros are in their element. Some make no secret of this and gloat to others about how much of a great time they're having indoors, much to Extros' dismay. Others simply possess a silent assassin-style demeanour, internally doing cartwheels and screaming 'Yaaaassssss!' within. It feels a little as though this is what

Intros have been waiting for all along. For too long now, they've been saying 'yes' to events and socials they have no desire to attend. This is the breathing space they so desperately needed – the chance to stay home without pressure, ignore the world outdoors and focus on their reading list, daily podcasts and list of homely activities. Intros must've baked enough cakes to feed the world's population should there be a mass, post-lockdown party.

How to Spot an Intro

Key phrases: 'I'm going within'; 'I've found so much to do at home'; 'This is my dream'.

Demeanour: A smug look and an outward glow. Shiny citizens whose permanent smiles are the bane of Extros' lives.

Lockdown Teachers

In some cases, it could be argued that these people have been hit the hardest. Teachers live by routine. Their day is structured by a series of lessons that begin and end at the wail of a bell. The same bells tell them when to start, when to finish, when to take a break and when to eat. They've now been taken out of their natural environment and effectively given full reign in the home.

Some may argue this is too much freedom all at once, but I passionately believe teachers have this covered. I've personally witnessed, first-hand, just how resourceful they can be. Teachers can perfectly plan pub meets after their last lesson is done or book has been marked. One day I witnessed Dave, the maths teacher, multitask brilliantly. He managed to run a virtual lesson via Zoom teaching the importance of algebra whilst sinking into his pint and swiping away on Hinge at the same time! All whilst on share screen, of course!

Not all teachers are as organised as Dave, however. Without the bell to remind them that lessons have begun, quite a few of my teacher associates are sleeping in past midday, which is effectively lunchtime for some teachers. Ridiculously early lunchtimes at some schools mean some teachers are on their second meal before most people have finished breakfast! It's a huge culture shock.

I've got to be honest, I've been a shoulder to cry on for many of my teacher friends who've cried claiming to miss the incessant requests and demands of young people like Jayden asking, 'Shall I underline the title, Miss?' for the fourth time, Mohammed pretending he hadn't pushed to the front of the lunch queue or Yasmine asking, 'Can I read, Miss?' before she butchers your PowerPoint presentation. 'The colours on the PowerPoint don't work, Sir. Green and yellow work better.' Oh, how the teachers have mourned these interactions. Lockdown Teachers have taken the longest to adjust but, in fairness, they're just happy they can now work without having to wear shoes (have you seen how many pairs of shoes teachers have under their desks?)

How to Spot a Lockdown Teacher

Key phrases: 'I miss them'; 'I remember when {insert appropriate name} said …'; 'I missed my online lesson today'; 'The bell didn't ring!'

Demeanour: Has a somewhat dishevelled look like someone who's just stepped out of a bunker. You can often spot these teachers looking for students under their pillows and waiting for the bell to ring.

Lockdown Dream Team

The Lockdown Dream Team have got it sorted. They know what it's about. They prepared for this like months ago and have full supplies, board games at the ready and a garden for the kids to play in. They're the ones flooding your social media timelines with pics of them sitting down to a perfectly cooked healthy dinner, playing family monopoly,  playing footie in the garden and doing science experiments at home. This couple seem to always be smiling, but what we don't know is that the little one just s**t in the paddling pool and the cat butchered a wood pigeon in the garden. These positive rays of sunshine keep the rest of us going and remind us of the importance of teamwork through a crisis.

How to Spot the Dream Team

Key phrases: 'We've done so much today'; 'Which project shall we work on next?'; 'Shall we do a family shop online?'

Demeanour: Proud, positive and perky, accompanied with the perfect selfie smile for all occasions.

The Homeschoolers

Homeschoolers are divided into two groups: 1), the group that has schools that have set up online classes, online resources and enough work for a child on a full-time shift at Sainsbury's and, 2), the group who've been left stranded in deep waters to navigate their child's education by themselves. The homeschooling thing works well if, a), the child has work to complete, b), access to technology and, c), tools like Show My Homework. Homeschoolers don't take, 'I've lost my login details!' as an excuse. They can recover their password easily by entering their email and recovering the password (just so you know!). However, those without access to computers would've found this time really challenging. I've had to advise many to get in touch with their child's teachers to find an alternative method.

Now there are many factions and divisions within these groups. Some have been waiting for this moment all their lives and others are buying trophies and medals for teachers as we speak. In this section, I want to share with you the two major groups within this category.

Group 1: AKA The 'On Its'

These are keen Homeschoolers who've set up online Zoom calls with other kids, created resources, organised home economics lessons in their kitchens and are teaching their children how to count toilet paper sheets and divide them by the number of people per household so they can predict when they need to stock up again online! These are the proactive parents and guardians who've embodied the patience of Poppins and secretly believed the teachers didn't know what they were doing all this time.

Group 2: AKA The I Can't Hack This!

A lot of these Homeschoolers are well known to the teachers already. They're constantly calling up the school complaining their child isn't getting enough homework, the curriculum is crap or their precious son/daughter should never have received that detention on Tuesday. Now, they're getting a little dose of their own medicine. They're slowly finding out that Little Johnny is a pain in the classroom, does in fact 'play up', knows not just some but **a lot** of swear words and isn't afraid to use them, and when asked to focus on a maths problem for ten minutes … well, forget it. Now these serial complainers are fast remembering all the times they've said, 'Well, he's not like that with me. The school must be doing something wrong,' and wishing the ground would swallow them up. A lot of them have already started penning their apology letters and, in the spirit of the comedienne Judi Love (you must watch her video 'Dear Teachers' at *www.tinyurl.com/judilove*), have confessed to finding a new appreciation for teachers and are begging for them back. But the teachers are not coming back, and Little Johnny can never seem to find Miss Green's online classes but, somewhere deep in his heart, he wants her to come back too.

How to Spot a I Can't Hack It!

Key phrases: 'I think you should try Google'; 'I don't get it'; 'We didn't learn it that way in school'; 'Go ask your brother'.

Demeanour: A posture and expression of fear, panic and dread as they wait to shield themselves from the next attack of complicated questions followed by, 'Mummy/Daddy {insert appropriate name} why **don't** you know? My **teacher** knows.'

Lockdown Life Coach

Lockdown Life Coaches are stressing a lot of people out. They mean well, but their well-meaning suggestions are often not welcome – these coaches are churning out endless videos and relentless content, delivering TED-style talks whilst doing a handstand and telling everyone else they should be clearing out their chakras and learning a new language. Lockdown Life Coaches are saturating Facebook and Instagram with posts telling, and in some cases lecturing people to, 'Stop feeling depressed and deflated and get out there: evolve, change, find a new hobby and grow.'

Whilst I personally believe this is a great time for us to reflect and do all that self-discovery, it's not for everyone, and what's needed more is compassion. Many people have lost their jobs, feel purposeless, contracted illnesses and lost loved ones. Some people are fighting their own demons and others have simply lost motivation whilst adjusting to this upheaval. The last thing they need is to feel pressurised to move, move, transform, transform, grow, grow! Sometimes people need to give themselves or be given permission to just 'be'. Now, there are many astute and compassionate Lockdown Life Coaches who get this, and that's beautiful to see, but it's the pushy ones that have taken over. The ones telling us to 'snap out of it' and who post memes that say, 'If you don't come out of Lockdown with a new skill, your side hustle started or more knowledge, you never lacked time, you lacked discipline.' How's that helpful when humanity is living through a global pandemic? Never before in modern history has the world been in such a situation. Global lockdown. Overnight, the way we live life has effectively come to an end and may never go back to normal. What's needed here isn't only compassion but also guidance and reassurance as people adjust to this incredible change.

How to Spot a Lockdown Life Coach

Key phrases: 'Learn a new language'; 'Find a new hobby'; 'Stop procrastinating'; 'Clear out your chakras NOW'; 'You will never get an opportunity like this again'.

Demeanour: Eager and excited. Grand gestures. Convoluted phrases and sentences. Larger than life.

The Working-From-Home Crowd

T his is a whole new world for some of these people. Many would've spent their entire adult lives working in offices in corporate buildings, bustling cities and conglomerate businesses. Now they finally get to look through the window at the outside world instead of that one-night stand across the office floor that they'd rather forget. Now they

can watch an episode of *Power* on mute whilst taking that sales call. Total freedom.

But what a lot of them don't realise is that with great freedom comes great responsibility. One cannot just take advantage. Those conference meetings must be attended, those minutes must still be taken, and those targets must still be met. Never before in history have there been so many office workers attending meetings dressed only from the waist up! Some have felt like they've found a whole new level of honesty and power within the workplace and many have finally found their voice, especially in conference calls, where they can now tell their boss, 'Sorry, can you just mute yourself?' or, 'If you turn your camera off, we may be able to hear you better,' or 'The Zoom call cut us off,' before finishing that episode of *Power* in peace.

On a serious note, I'm a firm believer that if many in this group were to spend this time focusing on self-care, well-being and health, they may find themselves turning their backs on the corporate world, tapping into their suppressed gifts and skills and setting up retreats in Bali! Remember, I said it here first!

How to Spot One of The Working-From-Home Crowd

Key Phrases: 'I work from home now …'; 'This meeting is due to end in the next five mins … just in case we get cut off'; 'I'm really finding myself, I think'.

Demeanour: Strangely relaxed, fulfilled and look like they're on the cusp of discovering a whole new meaning to life.

The Lockdown Roadman

Women, just when you thought it was safe. Just when you thought it was okay to walk down the street without being accosted by, what we affectionately call 'The Roadman', we realise just how wrong we were. If anything, one thing we should all have learnt during this time would be how to be mindful of each other's space, show a little patience and slow down. Well, 'space', 'patience' and 'slow down' aren't in Lockdown Roadman's vocabulary. In fact, if anything, they're simply speeding up.

Ladies, you know the roadman I'm talking about and, if you don't, you're lucky! He's the one that stands on street corners or outside betting shops and newsagents waiting to find the exact right moment to screech any of the following at you: 'Pretty gyal', 'I like yuh eyes', 'Beautiful', or any variation of, 'Where yuh man?' These include: 'Why yuh no 'ave no man?', 'Yuh 'ave man?', 'Pretty ting like yuh no 'ave no man?' Or, if you look anything like me, you'll get personalised lyrics such as 'Browning, Browning[1]' which then progresses to 'Big batty gyal'. So no, somehow the Lockdown Roadman's chirpsing game doesn't seem to have been hampered by lockdown unfortunately, and I'm starting to wonder whether they were listed as 'essential workers' and we somehow missed that on the memo!

---

1   A West Indian phrase typically referring to a 'light-skinned' person.

Now what I've surmised after studying their habits is that, although the *frequency* of their lyrics may have decreased as there are fewer sensible people outside, the *intensity* has increased. It's almost like a panicked desperation to get a 'Lockdown Gyal' (gyal being his word not mine) as soon as possible. With this desperation, the laughter lines around the eyes appear friendlier and the lyrics have a certain softness to them. 'Hey beautiful' and 'Sweet gyal' sound lighter and leave a softer fragrance wafting in the air. However, the spell is quickly broken when he comes swaggering towards you for your number, breaking all manner of social distancing rules! This leaves women running for their lives, leaving Lockdown Roadman to wait patiently until its next victim walks out to buy some essential tampons.

So why are the lyrics softer and desperation levels intensified at this time? Well, simply because the Lockdown Roadman spends most of his time outside. He hasn't yet made his house a home. He can't cook, won't cook, misses his grandma's cooking and is so desperately willing to fast-track his single status to 'Lockdown' so that he can be off the streets, be taken care of and fed three full meals a day. Don't be fooled ladies. We're not 'Lockdown Gyals'!

How to Spot a Lockdown Roadman

Key phrases: 'Sweet gyal'; 'Hey gyal'; 'Yes gyal'.

Demeanour: Needs to make moves quick as he doesn't know where his next meal is coming from.

Lockdown Lifers

I'm lucky enough to have a strong set of friends but when crisis hits, this is when you truly find out who your Lockdown Lifers are. These are the ones you turn to when you feel lost, uncertain, scared or lonely. Lockdown Lifers are those you call up to have pointless conversations about what you ate and how many dishes you've made with cabbage.

They'll listen intently. Why? Because neither of you have anything else to do on whatever day of the week it is! No, really, it's because they love you and you love them. They genuinely care about your well-being and want to make sure you're okay.

Lockdown Lifers will be on your speed dial. They're there for video calls, socially-distanced walks, friendship, laughter, tears and the first to pull you up when you haven't attended your online Zumba class. These Lifers will be by your side during the most testing of times forever.

How to Spot a Lockdown Lifer

Key phrases: 'Have you eaten today?'; 'Shall we do an online course?'; 'What time shall we video call?'

Demeanour: Attentive. Loyal. Compassionate.

Lockdown Love

Now this group deserves a whole book of its own, but in the spirit of this particular one, I'll condense this down to a page. It feels to me as if the Divine Spirit has pressed an enormous pause button, grinding everything to a halt, and relationships haven't been exempt from that. Relationships and decisions have been laid bare and lockdown has been a huge catalyst for their evolution to another level. Lockdown has provided us with a great opportunity to assess our relationships, whether it's a call to couples' therapy, cementing greater love and commitment or, on the other end of the spectrum, led to a break-up or divorce. Let's have a look at the three main levels of evolution.

Long-Term Lockdown Lovers

ong-Term Lockdown Lovers have got it covered. They've been together for years – storm, hail, wind or snow can't slow them down. They're prepared for anything. This couple knows how to ride through anything. They understand the power of simply walking quietly into another room when an argument has reached its peak, as opposed to storming out. They know that in the face of a crisis, like Peter in the Bible, the best thing to do is to keep calm, stay still and ride it out. They've a settled routine that keeps them ticking over and interchangeable roles that intuitively kick in depending on lunar cycles and moods. This couple is in tune and the outside world cannot interfere with their love waves. They have plenty of activities to do together – quiet nights on the sofa with Netflix, lazy walks in the park and sit-down-at-the-table dinners.

How to Spot a Long-Term Lockdown

Key phrases: 'We'll get through this together'; 'Shall we do a shop darling?'; 'Shall I get you a cuppa?'

Demeanour: A contented smile. Settled. At peace. Sometimes a little smug.

Lockdown Newbies

These are a curious bunch – their relationships are 'make-or-break' during times of crisis. When the government announced lockdown, this couple was left in a quandary. No dates allowed. No more cosy chats in restaurants, cuddles in the cinema or dinner for two at each other's houses. The rug, in that one announcement, was instantly pulled from their feet.

'What now?' they asked each other. Some boldly made the step to move in together, others put their relationship on hold, whilst others moved to more creative and innovative ways of keeping love, or lust, alive. Virtual dating with WhatsApp video calls, Facetime and Zoom replaced the real thing. Dating app statuses and profiles flipped from 'not into timewasting or endless penpal-style messaging' to 'looking for a socially-distanced penpal whilst in quarantine' and 'favourite places' quickly became Houseparty or WhatsApp.

Some of these Lockdown Newbie Lovers who took the bold step of moving in together have made it work. I've personally heard stories of how some have worked so well that it's brought them closer together. You never know, I may soon have to order my hat online in preparation for an online wedding! There have also been reports that this time inside has been like a 'free couples' therapy' with nowhere to run or hide. Some of these new couples have been forced to find ways of settling their differences in a short time to keep a harmonious household.

However, not all Lockdown Newbie Lovers have been experiencing the same joy. After two weeks of very sweet Netflix-and-chill moments, some hard cold facts have kicked in. Those endearing traits have disappeared as fast as toilet paper from the supermarket shelves. 'Dang! I'm dating a dude who doesn't even wash his rice or chicken and can't change a light bulb.' 'My girl ain't washed for days and there's no escape.' The arguments start, cracks appear and soon they grow into great, big, gaping craters. But what to do? The commitment has been made and there's no turning back. It's truly make or break, because watching your hot girlfriend being forced to remove her nails, five-day lashes and weaves will either leave a man traumatised for life or understanding what true love is.

How to Spot a Lockdown Newbie

Key phrases: 'Shall we Netflix and chill babe?'; 'What, you wanna go at it *again*!'; 'You're not who I thought you were!'; 'Never again'.

Demeanour: In the ones that make it – a smug smile and knowing look of 'we've got this'. For the ones that break it – forced, strained smiles with a facial expression that says, 'How do I get out of here?'

Lockdown Situs

Lockdown 'Situs' (aka situationships) have had to be the hardest hit during this time. Now I'd say these constitute 99 per cent of the 'complicated' statuses on Facebook. 'Complicated' simply means where one party is involved with someone who's already in a relationship,  but one they allegedly 'can't get out of'. It's a constant game of push and pull, with the attached party having most of the control in their 'complicated' situation. Situationships can look like relationships but, in reality, one party is in love with a player. Situationships are not just a case of, as commonly reported, 'The Man, His Wife and His Side-Chick', but can also be 'The Man, The Woman and her Lovers'. Thanks to Jada Pinkett-Smith, there's now a new term available for us all to use at will. 'Entanglement' is fast becoming attributed to a lot of relationship descriptions, and I'm sure it won't be long before it's officially recognised as a box to tick on official and legal documents. Entanglements are just that: complicated, messy, sticky situations were many wires are crossed, games played and hearts broken.

Situationships usually leave one party out in the cold, especially in situations like lockdown. This is when reality sinks in, skeletons creep out of the closet and drama comes to the fore. Those in long-term situationships with someone they believed was single or was staying 'because of the kids' are baffled as to why they didn't just make the commitment to move in. 'I just need my own space' isn't cutting it any more. Protests of 'We're in the middle of frickin' pandemic!' or 'It's been four years!' fall on deaf ears as Mr/Mrs Player is happy on-lining his situationships to virtual dates and multiple video calls from the comfort of their home.

Meanwhile, the attached party suddenly becomes, 'Busy with work' when really they're at home playing happy families, all the while warding off and fire-fighting the third party, their heart skipping a beat each time their beloved asks, 'Who was that?' Nowhere to run, nowhere to hide. What's done in the dark must come to light!

How to Spot a Lockdown Situ

Key phrases: 'Babe, why do you only call me when you're out at the shops?'; 'Who's that in the background, babe?'; 'It's just the TV. You paranoid boo'.

Demeanour: The one on the receiving end of the deceit has a questioning tone accompanied with raised eyebrows. The one spinning the lies has a high-pitched defensive tone. Eyes dart quickly from to side-to-side as if constantly on the lookout for danger.

LOCKDOWN ACTIVITIES

So, during this pandemic, we've had to redefine the term 'Lifestyle & Leisure'. With our daily routines out the window, we've been forced to navigate new territory and, with that, indulge in new activities or perhaps approach the same ones in different ways. Either way, it's forced a lot of us to think outside the box and, in other cases, brought us back to a simpler way of life. Here are some common activities that have taken place during this era.

The Lockdown Chirpse

This is The Lockdown Roadman's favourite activity. It gets him out the house and injects a little bit of normality back into his life. Think of it a little like going on safari. The Lockdown Roadman waits patiently, a little longer than he's used to mind you, for signs of activity 'on road'. He's usually the first one out, so he sees the elderly and key workers doing their shopping during their designated hour with the hope that a few younger carers or relatives pop up in the mix. When he spots them, his eyes bulge like binoculars have suddenly grown from the back of his head. On spotting his prey walk through the automatic doors of Iceland, he channels his inner lyricist and opens proceedings with, 'W'appen baby?' or 'Alright darlin.' Invariably, no one responds, but not one to give up easily, on the way out, it's either, 'Those bags look 'eavy' or, 'You 'ave man on lockdown?'

I mean, telling someone their bags look heavy with no intention of helping, especially with social distancing rules, is just rubbing it in! It's been noted, though, that a lot of Lockdown Roadmen have started chirpsing with their eyes, as social distancing makes it challenging to clearly hear and therefore respond to lyrics … as if anyone would respond anyway. I mean, there are only so many times someone can say, 'Pardon?' without it all falling flat and being rendered pointless. Lockdown Roadman is also having a hard time trying to get a woman to give him their number, as nobody wants to get close enough to him to give it. Or maybe they just don't want to in the first place! Life for the Lockdown Roadman is tough at the moment, but one thing we can say about him is that he's committed to his craft. He'll be there come sunshine, rain, storm or pandemic!

Lockdown Dating

The face of dating has changed and many more women on dating apps are swiping right – more than ever before. Standards have dropped as the need for communication, any kind of communication, deepens. The guy who says he's 41 but looks 72 suddenly looks like Idris Elba, and many men convince themselves Ms Poser may be able to meet their intellectual needs. You would've thought more men would have perhaps taken the time to fill out their descriptions and profiles a little more beyond, 'Ask me and I'll tell you.' But, unfortunately, it's been quite the opposite. More and more have flooded the apps during this time with not even a photo, thinking that surely there'd be some desperate woman out there who would DM a man with a name like 'bobsyourman' with a), no profile and, b), no profile pic. Others have pushed out the boat and added a photo or two, hoping to find a lockdown date on looks alone!

Some have become super-creative during this time, and that's been great to see. I've had conversations with friends who've had a Saturday night date in their living room starting with an innocent glass of wine and progressing to the bedroom three hours into the date! Some have concocted virtual backgrounds on Zoom, like tropical dates in the Amazon or romantic dates at the top of the Eiffel Tower or The Shard, whilst conversing with their date about the new recipe they tried for lunch.

Whether we like it or not, the way we date has changed rapidly, and it will either make us more creative souls or appreciate the preciousness of real human connection. You can touch someone with your voice, laughter, words and support, but a soul is something that can only be felt when in the full presence of another.

Lockdown Shopping

Having witnessed the madness in the shops before the lockdown announcement, I understand the importance of treasuring the food we buy. Realising that my quiet local shops were now too becoming invaded by the 'toilet paper and pasta thieves', I ventured out to the supermarkets. Never again: police in Iceland; queues the size of an army parade; empty shelves looking as though they've been attacked by vultures; hand sanitiser going for five times the price; delivery drivers getting accosted for toilet paper outside Sainsbury's. It was after this trip and after the online shopping I'd ordered three weeks previously was cancelled, that I locked myself down. The chaotic behaviour of the people panic buying brought on full-on anxiety.

Fast forward four weeks …

For some of us, going to the shops is fast becoming the highlight of our lives. It's like we deliberately forget that loaf of bread, just so we can pop out again, join our local socially distancing queue and interact with a human over the counter again.

There are a lot of interesting things people can observe whilst going to the shops:

- People wearing masks whilst rolling eyes at other humans that appear to get too close, all the while tapping their pin number, without gloves, into a card machine that's been touched more times than the Fontana del Porcellino statue in Florence!
- Lockdown Roadman lying in wait for his next chirpse, practising his lyrics and finding ways to break the social distancing codes.
- Halves of situationship 'couples' sneaking a phone call in before creeping home to wifey or hubby.

- People crossing the road, avoiding all eye contact as you walk happily down the street forgetting we're in the middle of a pandemic, which doesn't mean, by the way, you can't smile and greet each other. Take a breath and smile at them anyway.
- Those who enjoy a little chat about the weather, books they've been reading or where they got their African print mask from.
- Neighbours having a socially distanced chat, sitting on stoops and stairs or talking across their gates, fences or hedges.

All in all, it's a wonderful way to observe people whilst still feeling part of a community. A little trip to the shops is the new 'social club' now, so why not get your pen and paper out and journal the characters you see!

Lockdown Lunch

Lockdown Lunches are a serious matter. Having experienced what now feels like a distant nightmare in West Norwood High Street, I vowed to only shop in my local Budgens, newsagents or order online. Ordering online didn't come without its challenges. The once easy and accessible Riverfords and Abel and Cole frequented by people like me who are into organic and homegrown food, became flooded with regular Asda and Iceland shoppers who'd discovered these online gems in the midst of the pandemic. They were invaded to death by ex-supermarket looters, so much so that regular customers could hardly get a look in.

When I finally received my online order from my usual Riverfords and a new company called Fruit4London, I found myself with *a lot* of cabbage! Having worked so hard to seek out this food, like Frodo seeking the Golden Ring, I was reluctant to eat it! This meant a few uncomfortable moments staring at cabbages wondering what to do with them, but once I equipped myself with enough cabbage recipes to last a lifetime, progress was made.

Lockdown lunches are important. Now's the time to look after ourselves and truly eat the things that are good for our mind, body and soul. What we put into our body, especially now, will determine our mental and physical health. We live in a fast-paced world where food can sometimes be an after-thought or a fast-food snack whilst we keep our busy lives on the go and health on the back burner.

I can't tell you the number of dishes I've made using cabbage, spinach, kale and chickpeas. It may be fair to say that some of us have never done as much cooking in our lives as we have during this time! What's been your favourite lockdown lunch?

Lockdown Snacking

Please note that Lockdown Snacking is very different to Lockdown Lunch. A very different thing entirely. Whilst some of us have managed to implement new and healthier ways of eating, the reality for a large percentage of the population has been the opposite. Frequent trips to the fridge meant that eating habits went out the window for so many. The concept of structured meals such as breakfast, lunch and dinner lost its meaning as the eating regimen for the day morphed into a continuous day of grazing, with no beginning, middle or end. Thrice or four-times-a-day trips to the fridge became hourly visits, and the biscuit tin has never seen so much action.

Most of us started with good intentions. Staying at home meant we no longer had to rely on buying food on the go or over-indulge in expensive meals and takeaways, right? Some of us drew up healthy eating plans and promised to eat three meals a day and cook our way through the pandemic, yet we somehow ended up on the other end of the spectrum stuffing our faces with unhealthy snacks and dining on Doritos and doughnuts.

Grazing galore meant that many people piled on the lockdown pounds, emerging from the pandemic with new bodies and an intimate relationship with their snack cupboard. And who can blame the Lockdown Snacker? Comfort eating can be a coping mechanism for many, and perhaps the fridge needed the company too?

Don't Rush Challenge

#dontrushchallenge

The The Don't Rush Challenge was an essential for some over lockdown, but so confusing for others. So what is the Don't Rush Challenge, exactly? It was a challenge many took part in using TikTok. Being in the Generation X category, I struggled with this too! TikTok served as the answer to surviving the pandemic for most millennials and Gen Zs. TikTok seemed like the place to go to create and watch endless streams of fun and quirky mobile videos, and feel temporarily better about the fact you weren't allowed out to meet with physical friends.

From the outside looking in, the #dontrushchallenge looked easy. I'd watched plenty of Gen Zs doing before-and-after make-up shots seamlessly edited together at the touch of a make-up brush. I'd watched each person throw the make-up brush to the imaginary person in the next shot, so it appeared they caught it. How hard could it be, right?

Well, things took a turn for the worse when I had a brainwave of creating a Don't Rush Challenge of my own. All videos were shot to Young T and Bugsey's *Don't Rush* track. I knew the lyrics by heart, googled 'how to make a Don't Rush Challenge', practised my dance moves and was ready to rock 'n' roll. Ladies and gentlemen, I hear you ask, 'What could possibly go wrong?' Before I answer, I want you to imagine you're living by yourself, are clumsy at the best of times and have to a) turn the music on at the exact time of b) pressing record on your mobile phone, which is stuck to your wall with Blu Tack

c) throwing a pen at yourself and catching it whilst dancing to Young T and Bugsey's *Don't Rush* in your hallway, sweating, on a hot summer's day in your dressing gown. Well, I tell you: a lot can go wrong! If you want the proof, here's your evidence! (*www.tinyurl.com/cdpdontrush*)

Suffice to say, after an arduous 58 takes, I managed to employ a wonderful work experience student to put together a Don't Rush Challenge of our own, featuring our wonderful authors. I think it can be safe to say none of us ever want to hear Young T and Bugsey's tune *Don't Rush* for a long while! (*www.tinyurl.com/cdpdontrushouttakess*)

Zoom Calls

How many of us can honestly say they knew about or had used Zoom before lockdown? But I bet now you don't know how you lived without it. Zoom became *the* way to hold online conferences, run online courses, set up virtual classes, communicate with friends and family and even carry out job interviews. I'd say in the battle of the conferencing platforms between Houseparty, WhatsApp conference calls and any others that were out there, Zoom has come out on top!

I've been able to turn my own three-week workshop for authors, 'The Power of Your Story,' into a six-module online course. However, using Zoom has not come without some mishaps. Some of us have had unfortunate incidents occur on this platform, like 'zoom bombing'. In the middle of a meeting, the platform is invaded by trolls who've nothing better to do but to ridicule, humiliate and abuse others. In some cases, they hijack the screen to share porn, spout racial hatred and draw willies on the screen mid-conversation. This can be avoided by locking your meeting room, ensuring your meeting is password protected and by having a waiting room so that the host can only admit those invited. The upset and in some cases trauma this has caused people has been unacceptable, and I hope Zoom sorts this out asap!

Others have had unfortunate incidents like accidentally having their video camera on whilst having a 'quickie', traumatising their colleagues whose muted protests go unheard. Parents are not exempt from embarrassment either. Many parents have been exposed by Little Johnny asking inappropriate questions in the midst of an imperative meeting like, 'Mummy/Daddy, why do you always drink whiskey when you are on the laptop? You've had five now!' Or 'Mummy/Daddy, why aren't you wearing any pants?' whilst the rest of the team pretend not to hear.

Experienced 'teleconferencers' who've been doing this for eons are wondering what all the fuss is about. They're experts in holding meetings in their best blouses and swanky suited top halves whilst wearing pyjama bottoms and fluffy bunny slippers.

Despite the dramas, there are perks to Zoom. It's a wonderful way to connect with people, and basically keep business going as usual. If used correctly and when security is enforced, it's a great platform to use. Church services can now be held globally, global meditations have taken place and there are so many functionalities to implement for entrepreneurs, businesses owners, employers and employees and for people who just want to connect.

Revolutionising Your Biz

A lot of people have used this time to really change the way they run their business. And there's no harm in that at all because, sometimes, we must reassess old ideas, concepts and services, look at them with fresh eyes and see where we can adapt to flourish and grow. There's always room outside of the box. The buzzwords and phrases around this subject have been 'pivot', 'digitalise' and 'embrace technology'. It's been a perfect time to reflect on what was working but now no longer does. Business owners have had to adapt to a new climate and provide more value and service to our customers in new and innovative ways.

Many people have started online courses and training and there have been more podcasts than ever before. People are teaming up and creating joint ventures, running webinars and online workshops together and interviewing each other, all the while leveraging from each other's following. This, to me, is what entrepreneurship should be about – uniting, collaborating and supporting. I hope to see more of this continue way after this period comes to an end.

Learning a New Language

Lots of people have taken this time to learn a new language. Multilingual for some no longer means fluent in double Dutch and English, because now people are adding Swahili, Spanish, Portuguese and Yoruba to their repertoire. Apps like Duolingo, Busuu and Babbel have seen a surge of new customers seeking to learn new languages. Personally, I hope this means we'll have fewer Brits crossing waters expecting the citizens to speak English every time they arrive!

Self-quarantine is the perfect time and space to learn a new language from the comfort of your home whilst imagining a stroll down the streets of Paris or bartering in markets in Marrakech when all this is over. Communication is the key to human connection, so now is a perfect opportunity for us to brush up on our communication skills, challenge ourselves and embrace new cultures and languages so that we can have an even greater appreciation for others all over the world.

Unleashing Your Creativity

Arts and crafts have been another beautiful way to keep occupied and engaged during quarantine. There's something so therapeutic about creating art during this time and actually having the time to do it. We are beings who are designed to create and produce wonderful things, yet how often do we harness our creative abilities? As a child, I loved to make collages out of whatever I could find. I remember spending an entire day creating a collage made of old hairclips and bobbles. The joy that little things like this can bring should never be underestimated. We've been so used to exercising the right side of our brains – which governs order, logic and routine – that some of us have forgotten to embrace our creativity, colour outside of the lines and create something out of nothing. It's time to get those colouring pencils, paints, felt-tips, beads, mandalas and material out. I jest a little when I speak of the Lockdown Life Coach, but there's some truth in what they say – if you have the time to pursue a new hobby or revive one you've abandoned, now's the time to reunite with the creative in you!

Strengthening Our Immune Systems

Our immune systems are our natural defence system made up of a range of cells and organs that work together to protect the body. Strengthening our immune system is key to allowing us to ward off and protect ourselves from infections and diseases. Having a strong and healthy immune system makes us less susceptible to disease, which I call 'dis-ease', and creates an all-round healthy system in mind and body.

The importance of a healthy immune system is something that hasn't been widely covered in the mainstream media at all. Not so surprising, of course, but unfortunate because a real opportunity has been missed. It's only those who seek this information actively – those in the health and wellness industry and those who know and understand herbal and natural medicine – that brought the importance of a healthy immune system to the fore during this time.

Having said that, the health and wellness movement has had a huge surge in supporters and believers. I've never seen so many people adopt the regular morning ritual of a drink of hot water, lemon, turmeric, ginger and honey – something I've been doing for a long time. Lemon is rich in vitamin C, which is a natural antioxidant that contains anti-viral and anti-bacterial properties to strengthen the immune system. Turmeric is also a huge immune booster. Ginger is anti-inflammatory and so helps to boost the immune system too. It makes no sense to me why every household hasn't been given this information or why this isn't common knowledge. Other immune boosters are spinach, oranges, almonds, moringa[2] (known to contain more than 40 antioxidants and cited to have cured and treated over 300 diseases[3]) and sea moss (high in iron, magnesium, phosphorous and zinc). So many of these vitamins and minerals are beautiful for the immune system and can be bought as supplements, but the strength and function is so much stronger when consumed in its natural state, through food.

My desire is that, one day, every child and adult will be taught to understand the real benefits of eating to thrive rather than striving to eat, so that we're feeding our system instead of weakening it with low vibrational foods that simply destroy us.

---

2   https://restorativeblends.com/blogs/articles/top-7-health-benefits-of-moringa

3   https://www.sciencedirect.com/science/article/pii/S2213453016300362

Soul-Searching

So many of us are facing our shadows during lockdown. A lot of sh*t is rising to the surface and we're seeing things we've distracted ourselves from seeing in the past. So many of us have been 'busy', aka 'blindly unavailable to seek yourself'. We've been partying, working, engaging in meaningless relationships or flings, getting drunk, maybe even taking substances to escape from ourselves and our true essence. Some of us may have been wearing blinkers to our own shortcomings or failures and have been busy pointing the finger at others. One of the most apt quotes here is, 'When you point one finger, there are three fingers pointing back to you.'

Well those three fingers represent self-reflection and introspection, which is what we've all had an amazing opportunity to do during this time. My name, Daniella, means 'God is judge', which I love because it's a reminder that we cannot be defined or judged by another, not even ourselves. We may be able to discern what's a good or bad decision or what may even be wrong or right, but the judgement ultimately doesn't depend on someone else's opinion. My belief is that judgement isn't about punishment, but about the universal law of karma. The point here is that in the solitude of our homes, we can reflect and take responsibility for our choices, our words and our actions. And, in doing so, we can release ourselves from this judgement that has held us in bondage.

This is a great time to discover and ask those important questions:

- *Who am I really?*
- *What is important to me?*
- *Am I happy in and with my life? What do I need to change?*
- *What would make me happy?*
- *How can I be of greater service to humanity?*
- *What is my purpose here?*

These questions can really help with the process of soul-searching. Those self-isolating alone have been blessed with a wonderful opportunity in the quiet and solitude to really go deep. For how can we gain clarity in the chaos and the din of what we knew as 'normal life'?

Arguing

So, you've been stuck in lockdown with your family/partner/children/housemates for however long and, although you love them dearly, they're getting on your last nerve! This lockdown has you so stir crazy that if your child asks you for another biscuit, hubby asks what time lunch is or housemate insists on 'doing another online abs class', you're going to finally lose it. You're so sick to death of seeing the same faces peering eagerly at you expecting something, needing something and wanting your time and now the line between love and hate has become blurred.

Now you find yourself arguing so vehemently with your partner about whether tomatoes are a vegetable or a fruit (note-to-self, they're actually a fruit) or whether the 2012 Olympics ceremony was an orchestrated prediction or just a happy production, so vehemently that you now have to do a Google search on 'How to cheaply divorce my husband'.

You're so sick of having to explain to little Lottie that melons can't grow in your stomach if you swallow a seed, that you've been driven to consuming a bottle of White Zinfandel, then white rum, neat, just to cope with the backchat!

Your housemate, the one who was meant to leave just before all this happened, is still there. You desperately want your space and so have to resort to creeping around each other and apologising for being in each other's space. The only way to avoid awkward encounters is to take it in turns to use the kitchen, when not an isolated hermit in your room … in your own house. Did I mention this was the housemate who you did actually like at one point, but you now can't stand the sight of because she wants to spend every waking minute with you 'keeping positive' and 'doing activities'?

This is all stressing you out and you're finding yourself pulled into relentless arguments about nothing. My suggestion to you is to take time out for yourself. Be kind to yourself. If you feel things getting too much, do something for you: have a hot bath, go for a walk in the park, meditate, journal, pray or reach out to a friend or loved one. Your mental health is key.

Clapping for the NHS

Clapping for the NHS every Thursday evening fast became the new normal in the UK. No one can doubt the enormous investment, personal sacrifice and sheer effort the NHS and those that work for it have contributed to the UK. The NHS is the foundation of society, yet we all know, in no uncertain terms, they do not get the respect, honour or protection they deserve. I'm personally grateful for those doctors and nurses who put the health of the public first, risking their lives and sacrificing time away from their families to do so. Those doctors and nurses who work relentlessly to ensure patients get the best quality care are the bedrock of our society. My mother, a former nurse, was one of the many thousands of former and retired nurses who arrived in the UK during and after the Windrush era to build the foundations of the NHS, who were called back to serve once again during the pandemic.

The pandemic caused the NHS to be overstretched, overworked and understaffed. The outcry among the British public protesting against the treatment of NHS staff was resounding and unified. Lack of PPE and long unsociable working hours put many NHS staff on the frontline and vulnerable.

Rainbows were drawn on windows, walls and pavements; notes and posters were left on front doors and windowsills, and people signed petitions to show the public's support of the NHS. All of this paved the way to The NHS Clap!

The NHS Clap fast became a ritual in the UK, with thousands of people standing outside their front doors or in their windows, clapping, singing and whistling in support. Others banged unapologetically on pots and pans with spoons and rolling pins to ensure they were heard. This ritual brought tears to my eyes as I stood on the roof of my building showing support with my third-floor neighbour and eyeing up signs of life in the tower block ahead of me.

However this, though emotional at the start, soon became an excuse for some to a) socialise and grasp onto signs of life and human activity and b) a horrible exercise for witch-hunting and vilifying those not visible for 'The Clap'.

The 8 p.m. Thursday ritual, for some, became a 'Pavlov's dogs' exercise of jumping at the strike of the hour to drag out pots and pans and clap even if they felt like crap, because Nosy Nicky or Gossiping Greg would never let them forget it. There were reports of single mothers being dragged through the mud on mothers' forums and groups for not attending 'The Clap', with some even reaching the national media!

Despite this, the spirit of supporting the NHS did not crumble as, regardless of whether people made it to every event of 'The Clap' or not, we can all say each of us appreciates the selfless efforts of NHS workers, from the senior nurse to the NHS cleaner. They will forever be remembered and cherished. My only wish is that every clap they got would have been converted into the pay rise. These incredibly underpaid and undervalued NHS workers deserved better.

A special shout out here for the amazing 100-year old war veteran Captain Tom Moore, who raised a staggering £15m for NHS staff after reaching his goal of walking 100 laps of his garden. He is testament to the fact that individuals can do so much with collective support. Huge respect!

Sojourns in the Park

I've always been a nature girl and always find such beauty in green spaces. I'm lucky enough to have a local park that's pretty much deserted most of the time. Whilst I don't advocate sitting in crowded green spaces and sunbathing amongst thousands of other people, I'm one for getting out into nature as and when you can to heal the soul.

What has been wonderful about this time is that we can literally see Mother Nature restoring and resetting before our very eyes. The pollution rate has decreased significantly, the once murky canal in Venice is now so clear that dolphins and fish have been spotted swimming there, and even the parks seem to be glowing with joy in the absence of humankind. Nature is thriving as we take a backseat in our homes.

Visiting a park is a beautiful way to appreciate nature and connect with Planet Earth. Many of us have been living in a concrete jungle, running in the rat race called life, rushing to and from work, and we've forgotten to return to our essence, our natural state. For the past 11 years, I'd sit under my favourite tree when things got on top of me and reflect on the world around me. With all my 'busyness', I realised I hadn't visited the tree for years; in fact, I'd cut through the park many a time to and from work and, although I appreciated the trees on my journey, not once had I sat down to appreciate the beauty of a green space.

Now's the time to take that time. When you're next in the park, take the time to observe the trees. See how stable and steady their trunks are, how deep their roots go, how the branches and leaves sway and rustle to the flow of life with no fuss, no drama and no resistance. Observe how the flowers bloom and shine individually and collectively, with no competition. Observe how nature works in perfect synergy and unity, allowing all within it to grow and flourish. There's a lot we can learn from nature.

Volunteering

This is such an important time to come together. We're going through different experiences with our own individual and collective struggles. It's imperative we remember the elderly and vulnerable, those self-isolating alone due to illness or age, those on the poverty line, vulnerable children, those with mental health issues and struggling with isolation and those at risk of domestic abuse. Now more than ever we need to protect and look out for each other. So many organisations and voluntary groups have stepped up. One is the Mutual Aid Covid-19 Group that set up sectors in every borough in London to provide support to those in the community in self-isolation, the elderly, vulnerable or sick, in the form of food drop-offs, buddy systems and deliveries. Other organisations like Dare to Care Packages have taken on volunteers who helped with sending essentials to self-isolated people and PPE to the NHS.

There are plenty of ways to get involved. Many local charities have taken extra volunteers on board and can never have enough.[4] Some bigger charities, such as the Trussell Trust food bank network[5], have set up their own online schemes to match volunteers with food banks in their area. Local volunteer centres[6] and organisations such as Volunteering Matters[7] and Do-it[8] can match you up with charities

---

4   Information taken from The Guardian: Coronavirus and Volunteering 27th March

5   *www.trusselltrust.org/get-involved/volunteer*

6   *www.ncvo.org.uk/ncvo-volunteering/find-a-volunteer-centre*

7   *www.volunteeringmatters.org.uk/want-to-volunteer*

8   *www.do-it.org*

close to where you live. If you have specialist skills or areas of expertise such as IT, Reach Volunteering[9] will match you with charities that need your skills and expertise.

Volunteering and being a part of strengthening and caring for your community is a valuable way to spend your time. At a time when we may be feeling powerless and of little use, volunteering is a powerful way to reverse this feeling and enrich your community. Never underestimate the joy and support you can bring with the smallest of things you do.

---

9   *www.reachvolunteering.org.uk*

LOCKDOWN LESSONS: HOW CAN WE GROW AND CHANGE?

The world has faced a global crisis never before witnessed in the history of humankind. At one point, over half the entire world's population was in lockdown. It's safe to say that, after this, life will never be the same again. It would be a travesty to experience all of this and to have learnt nothing. There's so much for us to learn both as individuals and as a collective.

I'm a firm believer that there's beauty in the struggle and diamonds to be found in the gutter, and although it may seem like humanity has faced an insurmountable struggle, with this also comes the opportunity for growth and change for the better. Unplugging from the paradigm of fear and creating a new world together based on love and unity is my prayer for the world.

As we see Mother Nature flourishing, can we make the collective decision to flourish with Her? Can we make the collective decision to truly love our neighbours regardless of our differences? Can we extend love and kindness and be of service to humanity or will we continue to operate from an egalitarian mindset?

This section highlights just some of the ways in which we can grow and change. As *you* grow and change as an individual, you have the power to make huge transformations and shifts on this beautiful planet we call home.

Be of Service

The great thing about being of service is that each one of us can do it. As the late, great Dr Martin Luther King said, 'You only need a heart full of grace. A soul generated by love.' This pandemic has enabled us to reach outside of ourselves and really evaluate what's important. What hurt my heart the most during this time has been the actions of some people which were driven by the very opposite of love: fear.

Before lockdown was announced, it was as though 90 per cent of the nation had lost their minds. Supermarkets were raided as people delved into this 'stockpile' mentality, emptying shelves and leaving them bare for those who could only afford weekly shops or couldn't get there fast enough. My heart broke when I saw images of our elderly walking down empty aisles looking at shopping lists and wondering where the food had gone.

These are the very people we need to be looking out for and caring for. How can we ensure our elderly, vulnerable and those with mental illness are protected and safe at this time? What time can we give to helping our community? How can we have an impact on someone else's life? These are the questions we need to ask ourselves? Whilst we entered this world as individuals, we only survive as a collective. Each one of us is a much needed jigsaw piece in the puzzle of life. How can we eat happily in our own homes knowing that someone else down the road is starving?

Many people have had a little more time on their hands and so have invested it in volunteering, acting as buddies to the elderly and vulnerable, dropping off food and supplies and picking up prescriptions. Equally, those isolating need to be mindful too. I spent the majority of the start of lockdown risking my life getting essential bottles of Wray and Nephew, filter tips and scratch cards for my 'self-isolating shielder as a volunteer! I think my local newsagent thought I'd developed an alcohol and gambling problem during the pandemic.

On a serious note, being of service isn't always about how much you do – it's about the impact of what you do. Never underestimate the power of a smile. Your smile, your acknowledgement, your chit-chat with that person in the local shop could be the very thing that prevents someone from screaming at their kids when they get home, feeling isolated or even worse, taking their own life. We all have the incredible power to shine a little light on someone else's life through the smallest of actions.

Being of service is the greatest power we have.

Spend Time with Loved Ones

If anything, this period should've given us space to evaluate who and what is important to us. How many of us have fallen out with loved ones fighting over things we cannot even remember? How much longer can we hold a grudge? In times of crisis, we often reflect on who and what's important to us and put aside differences and old feuds, and now is as good a time as any to do so. Do we need to stay angry at Aunty Florence because she continually points out your perpetual singledom? Does your irritating brother really need your wrath right now because he read your diary two months ago?

Spending time with loved ones whether it's via video/phone call or in person enriches the soul. Humans thrive on connection, so making sure we're surrounded by loved ones who uplift us is crucial. One of the advantages of lockdown is that many families are spending more time together than they ever have. Whether you're a two-parent family with both parents working from home, live in a home that houses three generations under one roof, or a couple spending more time together than usual, you have a prime opportunity to nurture those relationships that we so often take for granted.

Lockdown ushered in new energy that allowed people to get back to basics with family dynamics. It was an opportunity to sit around the table together. Not separate from each other in different rooms, but together. It was an opportunity to have discussions, play board games, create inventive ways of staying occupied and being creative in the house. It was an opportunity for working men to truly appreciate the honest day's work of full-time mothers, or vice versa, whose work within the home is often discounted. It was an opportunity for couples to spend more time together, get to know each other on new and intimate levels and for families to bond together under one roof. So many of us are so busy rushing to commute to work only to travel home tired, and just about get through feeding the kids and ourselves before going to bed ready to do the same thing again the following day. We're constantly on auto-pilot and it's this mode that blocks us from being fully present and appreciative of the people within our lives.

Our relationships or family dynamics may not be perfect, but who do you need to reach out to today and build bridges with? Life really is too short.

Appreciate Nature

Now the temptation of pubs and cafés is gone, we're forced to recognise what we have. We're forced to appreciate what's natural, free and what's been nourishing us all along.

Nature has always been there. It exists, lives and breathes and asks for nothing. How many times have you walked through your local park and not taken the time to look at the shape of the trees, the colour of the leaves or notice the moisture that nourishes the grass? How long has this been here unnoticed and yet still it blossoms before our very eyes?

Over the last few months of lockdown, the green spaces we're blessed with have suddenly been acknowledged and appreciated. People have exchanged working in offices for taking a trip to their local park, laying down blankets, pitching up chairs and having socially distanced meets under the sun. It's a great chance to absorb vitamin D, connect with nature, connect with yourself and with friends. It's great to have a good old chinwag with a friend whilst being serenaded by birds and stroked by the sun. How often do we get to do this in our normal, day-to-day lives?

I've written enough about nature in this guide to lockdown, so I'll leave you with a quote I wrote 20 years ago at 20 years old, highlighting what we can learn from nature.

The Earth breathes, just as we do. The Earth feels, just as we do. The Earth loves, provides, forgives and nurtures. Even in the midst of devastation and inflicted destruction, it comes back. Even in the midst of attack, it comes back. It comes back to nurture us, to love us. It keeps on breathing, keeps on evolving, changing and remoulding. We can learn a lot from the Earth.

Connect with Self

The average person spends 2,340 hours per year working. That's, on average, 117,000 hours in a lifetime. How many of our hours do we spend developing ourselves, connecting with ourselves and just 'being'? How well do we truly know ourselves, or do we only know ourselves through the eyes of others? Can we really base our values or identity on the roles we play in life, our achievements and successes?

Some of us found lockdown hard as it meant being with ourselves. Away from the distractions, away from the drama, away from social lives, relationships and external forces that have been pulling on our energy for so long – the truth has been laid bare. Now's a great opportunity to go within. We're all we have.

Mental health is often perceived as a taboo subject but it's one that has become increasingly important to discuss openly. If we have a toothache, we go to a dentist; if we have any physical ailment, we go to the GP. So why wouldn't we seek help for our mental health? How many of us have been using work, social lives, and our duties to distract us from what's really going on within? Are we really happy in our lives or are we just playing a role? Our mental health and inner happiness is key to our well-being. That's true success.

In the 'busyness' of work, how well have we been looking after our bodies? I know that I'm not impartial to shoving down a sandwich, pain au chocolat or Jamaican pattie and not even noticing the taste as I'm scoffing in between boarding trains or switching classrooms at school. Are we taking the time to eat properly and nutritiously? Do we even know what foods and nutrients our body needs to thrive at its optimum or are we just eating for the sake of eating? Our bodies need to be filled with the right energy, vitamins and minerals so we can think clearly, have balanced hormones and chemical levels which affect our moods and state of mind, thus determining the quality of our daily experience. Can we use this time to understand our bodies better so we can have not only healthy bodies but also healthy minds? When our minds are healthy and balanced, we'll have more positive life experiences and therefore a happier life.

We can't expect changes in our lives if we keep holding on to outdated belief systems, patterns, programmes, ways of thinking and actions. Einstein is often attributed as having said, 'Insanity is doing the same thing over and over again and expecting different results.' He didn't say this but, whoever did (it's yet to be agreed), they're absolutely right!

Surround Yourself with Good Energy

Literary legend and Civil Rights activist, Dr Maya Angelou said, 'I've learned that people will forget what you said, people will forget what you did, but people will never forget how you made them feel.' In all her wisdom, she knew that it's not about a person's words or actions, but how they make you feel that's remembered. Now, more than ever, it's important to ensure we're surrounding ourselves with good energy and people who lift us higher rather than drag us down. We find ourselves in the middle of a passage of time where many of us feel uncertain, doubtful, powerless and sceptical. We may be questioning the motives and decisions of our leaders and organisations. We may be losing loved ones or questioning our own mortality. We're looking for a way out and a way to feel at ease again and this transition can be uncomfortable. It's vital to surround ourselves with people who are positive, empathetic, compassionate and understanding. Isn't it preferable to be around a Positive Petula than a Negative Nikesha?

Whilst it's totally normal to feel a little fearful and negative during this time, emanating that energy and passing it onto others isn't helpful. Who would you rather talk to – someone who's upbeat and uplifting or someone who's constantly reeling off 'death toll' numbers and saying we're in 'The End Times' of humanity? Personally, if I wanted to listen to someone quoting Scripture and telling me that none can escape the shadows of death or the pit of fire before us, I'd hang around outside Brixton Station or Speakers' Corner. What would you rather feed your mind? This period of time is challenging for all for so many reasons and it's perfectly okay to express fears and struggles; however what I'm saying is be mindful of the energy you release when you speak to others. People are looking for hope, positivity and solutions. Jim Rohn[10] said, 'You're the average of the five people you spend the most time with.' Make sure that the top five people you have on speed dial make you feel good – people with whom you can share your fears and doubts, can laugh and cry with and people who want to be part of building a better future with you.

---

10   American entrepreneur and motivational speaker

Check In on the Community

Mohammad Ali said, 'Service to others is the rent you pay for your room here on Earth.' We're all here temporarily. Our time here is finite. Earth has given us a beautiful place to live but we cannot exist alone. We're not lone islands nor are we nomads wandering the world alone, but part of a bigger framework intricately woven to complement each other. We are Humanity.

What's been beautiful during this time is to witness the real sense of community spirit and unification. At 20, I was lucky enough to spend a year in Tanzania, where the most widely used word is *karibu*, which means 'welcome'. President Julius Nyrere at the time had modelled Tanzania on a concept called *ujamaa*; a Swahili word for 'extended family' or 'brotherhood'. The belief behind this value is that a person becomes 'whole' only through the people or community. The spirit of thinking of 'others' or 'community' nurtures cohesion, love and service. This always resonated with me, as I'm a firm believer that we are our brothers' and sisters' keepers.

As humans we've always been tribal beings forming communities, groups and bands. In many African, Caribbean and Asian families, it's not uncommon to have three generations living under one roof (multi-generational households) or extended family close by. However, the average Western family dynamic is often nuclear[11] and we live in a society based on individualism as opposed to collectivism. We get swept away in the 'I am' and forget the 'We are'. Who are we without our neighbours, extended family and fellow mankind?

---

11 Comprising of two/one parent/s and child/ren

What I missed the most about Tanzania was the warmth of the people, the friendliness and easy conversation. You could jump on a *dala dala*[12] and by the end of it, everyone would feel like family. People who'd just met looked out for one another, fed each other and conversed together. It was a culture shock when I came back to London where we're afraid to look another in the eye, frequently escape from our bus seats to sit in empty spaces behind us to avoid the human sitting next to us to 'have space'. How many times have you been on a bus or train and noticed that bags have their own VIP seat whilst others are forced to stand? How did bags become more important than people?

It's been refreshing to see so many people contribute to the community through various volunteering schemes, community organisations and groups. It's been heart-warming seeing neighbours check in on each other and congregate, catch up and chat. Community is everything. Community means collective responsibility. According to Maslow's Law, our top need on his pyramid is to feel a sense of belonging. Community does this and, for some, community becomes the family they don't have.

Whose day can you light up today and how can you better serve your community?

---

12   Mode of transport in Tanzania equivalent to minibuses

Finances

Having to navigate finances during this era has been a nightmare for some. Many have fallen through the cracks of various schemes and initiatives and had to work harder than ever before.

Many who are self-employed, like me, lost freelance jobs and a regular income in one foul swoop, leaving us financially unstable and uncertain as to whether we'd be accounted for in the great financial pandemic. For many self-employed people and small business owners, watching their friends and family furloughed whilst their own financial situation hung in the balance was very difficult to sit through.

And if that wasn't hard enough, following Boris Johnson and his Chancellor Rishi Sunak's financial plan for the self-employed sometimes felt like following a drunken paralytic around *The Crystal Maze*. Tough! A lot of us struggled to wait until June and, after some time, some of us managed to receive the furlough they needed to stay afloat. Others took mortgage holidays and appealed to the better nature of landlords, while others suffered threats of eviction and long phone calls with HMRC and Universal Credit.

One thing that can be said for sure is that Universal Credit experienced more calls than ever in the history of humankind. A record of 500, 000 people applied in the first two weeks of lockdown. It was so bad, I'm surprised they didn't employ the first 1,000 applicants as customer service operators then perhaps, at least, someone may have answered the phone! In all fairness, Universal Credit have done an amazing job with their response to the astronomical increase in demand and I'm sure that Universe will credit their workers in abundance.

After some time, owners of small businesses were offered Bounce Back Loans under The Interruption Loan Scheme, whilst many self-employed people were also eligible for grants. Many of us faced an immeasurable level of stress before we were able to ascertain whether a), our businesses would be adversely affected, and, b), whether we'd be entitled to anything at all. The biggest lesson I've personally learnt from this has its roots in the Brownies' motto, 'Be prepared'. We must be prepared for anything and be ready to be adaptable so we can adjust to everything. Financial experts have always proclaimed we must have between three to six months of wages saved up for an emergency fund. This advice couldn't have been more crucial for a situation just like this.

For me, there has been one saviour in all of this: Martin Lewis from *www.moneysavingsexpert.com*. He managed to translate the schemes, initiatives, loans and grants on offer, break down what furlough meant for PAYE and self-employed workers and consistently give advice in a cool, collected and informative manner. Martin Steven Lewis: you've been the self-employed person's hero and we'll never forget it!

Be Adaptable

Benjamin Franklin said, 'Change is the only constant in life. One's ability to adapt to those changes will determine your success in life.' If there's one thing that's inevitable in life, it's change. Throughout history, it's been proven that those who are adaptable to change not only survive, but thrive. Observing the animal kingdom, the chameleon changes its colour to blend in with its environment, animals hibernate during the winter and, did you know Alaskan Wood Frogs can freeze 60 per cent of their bodies to survive temperatures down to −80 Fahrenheit? Nature has a wonderful way of adapting, and we shouldn't be exempt. We need to be like Alaskan Wood Frogs!

This era has ushered in a lot of change. With the majority of small businesses, schools and offices closing and events postponed, we've had no choice but to be adaptable to our environment. I can only imagine how hard it must be to work from home whilst homeschooling children at the same time and, although we've had a giggle about the difficulties in Part I, I salute those who rose to the challenge.

Although tough, this has been a great opportunity for us to develop new habits, build in new routines and rhythms that promote a better way of living and working. Has the change made you think differently about how you want to interact with your children or family? Has the change made you view your children differently as you find out how they learn? Will you now instil new ways of learning when lockdown is over? Will you take more of a role in your child's education? Perhaps you may even have seen some flaws in the educational system that need to be addressed?

For many of us entrepreneurs, it's been a time to really rework our businesses. In the space of a few short weeks, I had to teach myself how to use Zoom and other online platforms to convert my forthcoming workshop, 'The Power of Your Story', onto a digital platform and run innovative book launches online. Networking events have been replaced with digital meets, with the bonus being that people from all over the world can now attend! I've seen businesses thrive online and business owners consult other entrepreneurs on how to become more visible online and monetise their expertise. I'm being serious when I say I've fully adapted to just dressing from the waist up and enjoyed saving money on travel! I'll have no idea what to wear when events are on again. Some of us will need socialisation programmes and workshops (online of course!) and a reminder of who we were BL (Before Lockdown) before we venture out again, because the person I am now lives in tracksuits and dressing gowns. My bras and knickers are now foreign to me!

Joking aside, there's incredible power in adaptability. This ability to adapt will determine our success, just like the Alaskan Wood Frog. We must change with the climate, not wait for the climate to change. We must and continually learn, grow, evolve and adapt so that we can find a way to thrive in any given situation.

All of us in some way, shape or form have had to adapt to a new way of living and my only hope is that it helps us to look at old situations with new eyes, gives us the power to start eliminating the things that make us unhappy and start doing things differently.

Closing with Love

And so, whilst we've had a laugh about the Lockdown Roadman and Lockdown Life Coach, I wanted to also provide an opportunity for self-reflection and self-evaluation in between the funny moments. I believe that everything is divinely guided, and everything happens for its time, in its time, and this Great Pandemic/Lockdown period, or whatever term we wish to attribute to this unique passage of time, is no exception to that. There's beauty in every struggle and I truly believe this period has brought out the best and worst in humanity, and I consciously choose to focus on the best.

This period has taught me a lot about valuing life. Every day we get to wake up and make a different choice: to live and lead with Love and to be the best version of ourselves we can possibly be. We get to choose whether we want to be stuck in a routine we hate, get caught up in drama we don't need, speak our truth, live in purpose or see our neighbour as an ally or enemy. What we see in our outer world is merely a reflection of our internal state. Do we value ourselves enough to do the inner work? Can we value each other enough to create a greater change in the world; one that benefits us all and not just the few?

Can we do better? Can we *be* better? What does better truly look like?

So, whatever timeframe or timeline you're reading this in, whatever's happened or didn't happen, know that I love you and I'm wishing you well. Life is for living. Life is precious; live, love and laugh as if every day was your last.

Useful Organisations

Domestic Violence and Mental Health Support Organisations

Free Your Mind

Support individuals that have experienced childhood domestic violence and mental illness as a result.

🌐 *www.freeyourmindcic.com/*

Refuge

The freephone, 24-hour National Domestic Abuse Helpline

🌐 *www.nationaldahelpline.org.uk/*

📞 *0808 2000 247*

Skye Alexandra House

Skye Alexandra House is an organisation that provides services, training and guidance for vulnerable girls and young women.

🌐 *skyealexandrahouse.co.uk/our-story*

📞 *07944 480 782*

Maytree

London based respite centre that provides short-term respite to people who are suicidal. People can ring them directly to discuss arranging a stay. You can only stay there once.

 www.maytree.org.uk

 0207 263 7070

Mood Swings

Helpline proving advice, info and support to people with severe mood disorders

 www.moodswings.org.uk

 0845 123 6050

No Panic

Helpline for people with anxiety disorders. Also has telephone recovery group for members

 www.nopanic.org.uk

 0800 138 8889

Sane

Emotional support line for people in mental distress

 www.sane.org.uk

 0845 767 8000

Samaritans

24 hour helpline for

 www.samaritans.org

 08457 90 90 90

Childline

Free and confidential help for young people in the UK.

 www.childline.org.uk

 0800 1111

Voluntary Organisations

Trussel Trust

Support a nationwide network of food banks and provide emergency food

 www.trusselltrust.org

 01722 580 180

 Volunteer: www.trusselltrust.org/get-involved/volunteer

NCVO

Offer a Volunteer Centre Finder service. Volunteer Centres are local organisations that provide support and expertise within the local community to potential volunteers, existing volunteers and organisations that involve volunteers

 www.ncvo.org.uk/ncvo-volunteering/find-a-volunteer-centre

 0207 520 2414

Do-it

Offer a platform for volunteers to sign up to help the community and for voluntary organisations to find volunteers.

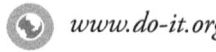 *www.do-it.org*

Volunteering Matters

Run over 80 UK volunteering programmes to help communities turn local knowledge and energy into action and progress.

www.volunteeringmatters.org.uk/want-to-volunteer

020 3780 5870

Reach Volunteers

Recruit volunteers and help organisations find volunteers

www.reachvolunteering.org.uk

0203 943 9901

Another Night of Sisterhood (ANOS)

Offer a wide range of services that aim to support families, children and young people within our local community.

www.facebook.com/ANOSisterhood

anosisterhood@gmail.com

Covid-19 Mutual Aid UK

A group of volunteers supporting local community groups organising mutual aid throughout the Covid-19 outbreak

covidmutualaid.org/

Thank you

Thank you to the Conscious Dreams Publishing team, who worked diligently and with commitment, helping to create this book.

To my editors, Rhoda Molife and Lee Dickinson, thank you for your hard work and scrupulous editing.

To my typesetter, Oksana Kosovan, thank you for your flawless typesetting and dedication.

To my illustrators, imaginabox studio and Rahmon, thank you for your awesome illustrations. Your talent and commitment are appreciated.

Last but not least, thank you to Jae Thompson for the cover art and Alaka Oladimeji Basit for the cover design.

No woman is an island, and it takes a dream team to make glorious things happen.

About Daniella Blechner

Daniella Blechner is an award-winning entrepreneur, founder of Conscious Dreams Publishing, author and Book Journey Mentor who lives in south London. Over the last four years, she has published more than 80 books, mentored 190 authors and aspiring authors, assisting them in transforming their powerful stories and messages into successful books.

Dubbed the 'class clown' in her former years, Daniella has always sought to bring joy and humour to other's lives and believes laughter is the best medicine in times of challenge.

Achievements include surviving lockdown alone, gaining 400+ comments on a post about what to do with cabbage during lockdown, completing the Don't Rush Challenge, living in Tanzania as a voluntary teacher whilst getting away with speaking broken Swahili and climbing to the top of Mt Kilimanjaro!

Daniella is also an English teacher with 11 years' teaching experience. Her conscious dream is that we get to create and live in a world that is founded on equality, love and unity for all.

Daniella offers free 30-minute consultations for anyone interested in writing a book, as she believes that everyone has a story inside, and the power is using it to positively impact another.

 www.consciousdreamspublishing.com

 daniella@consciousdreamspublishing.com

 www.consciousdreamspublishing.wordpress.com

Other Books by Daniella Blechner

Mr Wrong is an insightful and witty exploration into why some women continually attract the wrong men. This powerful collection of humorous, insightful, and entertaining stories are written by women from across the world that have encountered and overcome toxic Mr Wrong relationships. Featuring success stories and stories from men too, this book is a real journey of self-discovery.

Mr Wrong Workbook offers practical exercises, quizzes and reflections that will enable you to re-evaluate your values and priorities, assess your relationships and create positive changes in your life. We all make mistakes in relationships and blame and berate ourselves at times. How can we learn and grow?

7 Shades of Love is a beautiful collection of poetry that explores the universal theme of love combined with the Eastern and Western associations behind the 7 colours of the rainbow. This book is a unique approach to the ways in which these global poets, have dealt with love – the highest of all universal frequencies.

7 Steps to Creating the Greatest Version of You (for women) is a workbook designed to assist you in clearing away past hurt, focusing on our intentions and letting go of blocks so that you can tap into your Inner Guide and start painting a positive canvas for your life.

7 Steps to Creating the Greatest Version of You (for girls) Do you know the power you hold inside yourself? Do you know that you are unique, beautiful and powerful in every way? This book is designed to help raise the self-esteem, self-worth and positive identity in teenage girls just like you.

The Book Journey Mentor's Guide to Self-Publishing Guide and **Workbook** are comprehensive blueprints to publishing your book with ease and confidence. These guides will equip you with the knowledge you need to create, publish, distribute, promote and market your book successfully.

Conscious Dreams
PUBLISHING

Be the author of your own destiny

Find out about our authors, events, services
and how you too can get your book journey started.

Conscious Dreams Publishing

@DreamsConscious

@consciousdreamspublishing

Daniella Blechner

www.consciousdreamspublishing.com

info@consciousdreamspublishing.com

Let's connect

Lightning Source UK Ltd.
Milton Keynes UK
UKHW020633100920
369682UK00015B/1696